afternoon
tea
with *Bea*

afternoon tea with Bea

photography by Kate Whitaker

London New York

Designers Steve Painter and Barbara Zuñiga
Commissioning Editor Céline Hughes
Senior Production Controller Toby Marshall
Art Director Leslie Harrington
Editorial Director Julia Charles

Prop Stylist Steve Painter
Food Stylist Lucy Mckelvie

First published in 2013 by
Ryland Peters & Small
20–21 Jockey's Fields
London WC1R 4BW
and
519 Broadway, 5th Floor
New York, NY 10012
www.rylandpeters.com

The recipes in this book have been published
previously by Ryland Peters & Small in *Tea with Bea*

UK: 10 9 8 7 6 5 4 3 2 1
US: 10 9 8 7 6 5 4 3 2 1

Text © Bea Vo 2011, 2013
Design and photographs
© Ryland Peters & Small 2011, 2013

Printed in China

ISBN: 978 1 84975 420 0

Notes

- All spoon measurements are level, unless otherwise specified.
- All eggs are medium (for the UK) or large (for the US), unless otherwise specified. Uncooked or partially cooked eggs should not be served to the very young, the very old, those with compromised immune systems, or to pregnant women.
- When a recipe calls for the grated zest of citrus fruit, buy unwaxed fruit and wash well before using. If you can only find treated fruit, scrub well in warm soapy water and rinse before using.
- Ovens should be preheated to the specified temperature. Recipes in this book were tested using a fan-assisted oven. If using a regular oven, follow the manufacturer's instructions for adjusting temperatures. However, as a general rule, temperatures should be increased by about 15–20°C or about 35°F if using a regular oven.
- Use an oven thermometer. Most ovens are inaccurate by at least 20–25°C, which will affect the outcome of the cakes.

contents

time for tea

Choose some deserving friends, pick a date and send out the
invitations – then sit down and work out a winning menu for
your afternoon tea party!

Tailor your menu to your guests. If they have a very sweet tooth,
make some delicate marshmallows (page 50) or rocky road fudge
bars (page 34). If someone can't eat dairy, consider making them
some dairy-free biscotti (pages 30–33), or for a vegan party, pull
out all the stops and bake a vegan chocolate mousse cake (page 56).

Make sure that most of your menu can be prepared and made in
advance so that you are not trying to finish decorating a cake or
putting too-hot-to-eat cookies straight on the tea table when your
guests arrive.

If you want a centrepiece of stunning cupcakes, practise using a
piping bag and different nozzles/tips! You want to avoid wowing
everyone with your invitations and then presenting them with
disappointing, lopsided mounds of buttercream atop your cupcakes!

Use this book for inspiration as well as for the recipes. Mix and
match the fillings (pages 18–23) and basic cake mixes (pages 12–17)
to suit your tastes. Or use your own favourite cupcake recipe but
finish it off with one of the frostings on these pages. Good luck and
happy baking!

basics

making perfect tea

1   Always look for good, loose-leaf teas. Teas are made up of long leaves that are dried and processed. When whole, the essential oils are locked inside the tea and kept from oxidizing and tasting bitter.

2   Teas should be stored in an airtight, dark, cool container. Don't buy teas that come in boxes with open windows – the teas are already oxidized by the time you get them.

3   The trick with teas is to extract all of the lovely aromatics without extracting too many tannins, which cause bitterness. Match the temperatures and brewing times to your specific teas. Delicate teas like white or green teas require a lower temperature and longer brewing times; black teas will need a high temperature and slightly shorter brewing times.

4   Tea leaves need room to expand and move around. I recommend T-sacs, which are large, fillable bags because they're roomy and therefore suit teapots and mugs.

5   While loose-leaf teas can be expensive, the high quality of a tea means that the leaves can be infused over and over again. In fact, for many high-quality teas, the second, third and even later infusions are considered to be better than the first.

6   Recipe for tea: You will need 2–4 grams whole loose-leaf tea; 250 ml/1 cup filtered water; teapot; tea strainer for the cup; cup. Place tea inside the teapot. Boil the water and pour into the pot. For white tea, let the water sit for 1 minute before pouring into the pot, as you don't want it to be at boiling temperature. Let steep for 2 minutes (3 for white and herbal teas). You want to make sure the leaves have time to move freely to fully expand and release the proper aromatics. Strain into cup. Add milk and sugar or honey and lemon as desired.

making perfect coffee

1   Invest in freshly roasted beans from your local supplier. Beans shouldn't be any older than a few days old, and the expiration date on proper coffee beans is typically about a month.

2   Consider not just fairtrade: many artisanal roasters actually have better-than-fairtrade agreements with farmers.

3   Always buy beans whole – coffee beans have wonderful aromatic oils that are released when crushed, but the oils are also very fragile. Crushed too soon, the oils will dissipate and even worse, can go rancid. Coffee beans should be ground only a few minutes before use.

4   Invest in a burr grinder; those same aromatic oils in coffee can be spoiled by high-speed, uneven grinders. Invest in a good burr grinder, such as KitchenAid's Burr Grinder, or better yet, a Hario Skerton Coffee Mill that is just like a pepper mill, only for coffee!

5   Brewing times for coffee are just as important as baking times for cakes!

6   My preferred method for brewing at home is the lovely French press.

7   Recipe for coffee: You will need 500 ml/2 cups filtered water; 30 g/1 oz. high-quality filter coffee beans; French press (500-ml/2-cup capacity); cup. Start to boil the water. Grind the coffee beans using either an electric burr grinder or a manual one. You want a fairly coarse grind for filter coffee to allow for the extraction of the aromatics but not too much of the bitter oils. Pour into the French press. Add the boiling water. Stir for a good 30 seconds to let the coffee grounds swell up and release their oils. Add the lid. Let sit for 3 minutes, before gently plunging. Pour into cup. Add milk and sugar as desired.

almond frangipane cake

This base is used in the Frangipane Raspberry Cake on page 63. It requires almond paste, which provides a super-smooth consistency. Look for almond paste with a maximum of 50% sugar content plus just almonds (or marzipan if it's 50–60% almonds plus sugar). Lower-quality marzipan contains too much sugar, resulting in an uncake-like brick.

250 g/2 sticks butter, soft

5 tablespoons caster/superfine sugar

600 g/1 lb. 5 oz. almond paste (e.g. from King Arthur Flour or Anthon Berg Raa Marzipan, 60% almonds)

6 eggs

280 g/2 cups plain/all-purpose flour

1½ tablespoons baking powder

1 x 25-cm/10-inch or 2 x 18-cm/7-inch cake pans, greased and baselined with parchment paper

serves about 20

Preheat the oven to 160°C (315°F) Gas 4.

Using an electric mixer with paddle or beater attachment (or an electric whisk), beat the butter, sugar and almond paste until well combined. Slowly mix the eggs into the butter mixture, one at a time, until thoroughly combined and fluffy. Now beat for an additional 2 minutes.

Put the flour and baking powder in a large mixing bowl and sift twice. Fold into the almond mixture.

Spoon the mixture into the prepared cake pan and bake in the preheated oven for 35–45 minutes. A wooden skewer inserted in the middle should come out with almost no crumbs attached. Bake for an additional 5–10 minutes if necessary. Remove from the oven and let cool in the pan for 10 minutes. Slide a table knife all around the edge to loosen the cake, then remove from the pan. Transfer to a wire rack to cool for 1 hour.

almond tea cake

This cake can be served plain – it's so good that you'll find yourself having one slice, then another an hour later and by the end of the day you'll wonder where it all went.

240 g/1 cup plus 2
   tablespoons caster/
   superfine sugar

zest of 1 lemon

150 g/1 cup plus 1
   tablespoon plain/
   all-purpose flour

70 g/⅔ cup ground almonds

2 teaspoons baking powder

a pinch of salt

130 g/½ cup Greek yogurt

3 eggs

½ teaspoon vanilla extract

¼ teaspoon almond extract

80 ml/⅓ cup sunflower oil

50 g/3 tablespoons butter,
   melted

*20-cm/8-inch round cake
pan, greased and baselined
with parchment paper*

serves 8–12

Preheat the oven to 170°C (340°F) Gas 5.

Put the sugar and lemon zest in a large mixing bowl and rub with your hands until it smells lemony. Add the flour, almonds, baking powder and salt and mix well.

Put the yogurt, eggs and vanilla and almond extracts in a separate bowl and whisk until thoroughly combined. Add to the dry mixture and mix until just combined and no trace of dry flour remains. Fold in the oil and melted butter.

Spoon the mixture into the prepared cake pan and bake in the preheated oven for 28–35 minutes. A wooden skewer inserted in the middle should come out with almost no crumbs attached. Bake for an additional 5–10 minutes if necessary. Remove from the oven and let cool in the pan for 10 minutes. Slide a table knife around the edge to loosen the cake, then remove from the pan. Transfer to a wire rack to cool for 1 hour.

chocolate buttermilk cake

This has all the qualities you want in a chocolate layer cake – the chocolate mouthfeel, a buttery aftertaste, a fine, feathery crumb and a perfect density to stand up to any type of filling. It is the base used in the Triple Chocolate Cake on page 60.

225 g/8 oz. good dark/semi-sweet chocolate (we recommend 70%), finely chopped

65 g/4 tablespoons Dutch-process cocoa powder

175 g/1½ sticks butter

4 eggs

300 g/1½ cups caster/superfine sugar

175 g/1¼ cups plain/all-purpose flour

½ teaspoon bicarbonate of/baking soda

¼ teaspoon salt

235 ml/1 cup buttermilk

1 x 25-cm/10-inch or 2 x 18-cm/7-inch cake pans, greased and baselined with parchment paper

serves about 20

Preheat the oven to 170°C (340°F) Gas 5.

Put the chocolate and cocoa powder in a large, heatproof bowl.

Melt the butter in a pan over medium–high heat. Pour into the bowl of chocolate and cocoa and stir until melted and smooth.

In another bowl, whisk together the eggs and sugar. Pour into the chocolate mixture and mix until well combined.

Put the flour, bicarbonate of/baking soda and salt in a large mixing bowl and sift twice. Add one third of the flour mixture to the chocolate mixture and mix until well incorporated. Add half the buttermilk and mix until just combined. Repeat with another third of the flour mixture, then the rest of the buttermilk. Finally, add the last third of the flour mixture and mix until combined.

Spoon the mixture into the prepared cake pan. Bake in the preheated oven for 35–45 minutes. A wooden skewer inserted in the middle should come out with almost no crumbs attached, and the middle of the cake, when pressed, should spring back slightly instead of sink. Bake for an additional 5–10 minutes if necessary.

Remove from the oven and let cool in the pan for 10 minutes. Slide a table knife all around the edge to loosen the cake, then remove from the pan. Transfer to a wire rack to cool for 1 hour. Cut in half horizontally and fill with frosting of your choice.

wheat-free Valrhona cake

This recipe is actually adapted from a lovely chocolate fondant recipe I learned at Nobu restaurant. Slightly tweaked, it becomes a wonderful wheat-free alternative with a great crumb and magnificent texture, something sorely lacking in most flourless cakes.

250 g/9 oz. Valrhona Araguani 72% Dark Chocolate, Scharffen Berger 70% or Green & Blacks Organic 70%, finely chopped

250 g/2 sticks butter

5 eggs

2 egg yolks

100 g/½ cup caster/ superfine sugar

30 g/3 tablespoons rice flour

30 g/3 tablespoons natural cocoa powder

20-cm/8-inch round cake pan, greased and baselined with parchment paper

serves 8-12

Preheat the oven to 170°C (340°F) Gas 5.

Put the chocolate in a large, heatproof bowl.

Melt the butter in a saucepan over high heat. Pour into the bowl of chocolate, stir until melted and smooth and set aside.

Using an electric mixer with whisk attachment (or an electric whisk), beat the eggs, egg yolks and sugar until pale and creamy in colour and quite thick – almost like a soft whipped cream.

Gently fold the egg mixture into the chocolate mixture.

Sift the rice flour and cocoa powder into the bowl and fold into the mixture.

Spoon the mixture into the prepared cake pan and bake in the preheated oven for 28–35 minutes. A wooden skewer inserted in the middle should come out with almost no crumbs attached, and the middle of the cake, when pressed, should spring back slightly instead of sink. Remove from the oven and let cool in the pan for 10 minutes. Slide a table knife all around the edge to loosen the cake, then remove from the pan. Transfer to a wire rack to cool for 1 hour.

vegan chocolate cake

It's vegan but we don't tell people it is and they love it. That's how good it is. This is the base for the fantastic Vegan Chocolate Mousse Cake on page 56.

275 g/2 cups plain/ all-purpose flour

100 g/¾ cup natural cocoa powder

2 teaspoons bicarbonate of/baking soda

1 teaspoon baking powder

a pinch of salt

450 ml/1¾ cups soya milk (e.g. Bonsoy or other unsweetened soya milk)

2 teaspoons red wine vinegar

320 g/1⅔ cups caster/ superfine sugar

320 ml/1¼ cups sunflower oil

2 tablespoons vanilla extract

23-cm/9-inch round cake pan, greased and baselined with parchment paper

serves 8–12

Preheat the oven to 160°C (315°F) Gas 4.

Put the flour, cocoa powder, bicarbonate of/baking soda, baking powder and salt in a large mixing bowl. Sift twice.

In a separate bowl, whisk together the soya milk, vinegar, sugar, oil and vanilla extract. Pour into the flour mixture and stir until well combined.

Spoon the mixture into the prepared cake pan and bake in the preheated oven for 40–55 minutes. A wooden skewer inserted in the middle should come out with almost no crumbs attached, and the middle of the cake, when pressed, should spring back slightly instead of sink. Bake for an additional 5–10 minutes if necessary.

Remove from the oven and let cool in the pan for 10 minutes. Slide a table knife all around the edge to loosen the cake, then remove from the pan. Transfer to a wire rack to cool for 1 hour.

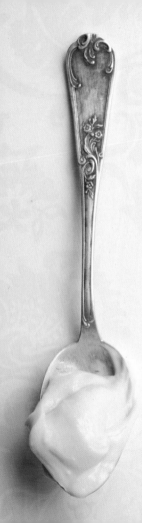

vanilla pastry cream

This pastry cream is thicker than the typical English custard, making it suitable as a filling for cakes.

250 ml/1 cup milk

3 tablespoons caster/superfine sugar

2 egg yolks

2 teaspoons vanilla extract

1 tablespoon cornflour/cornstarch

35 g/2½ tablespoons butter

makes 375 g/13 oz.

Put the milk and half the sugar in a medium saucepan over medium heat and stir with a wooden spoon. Bring to a boil. As soon as it comes to a boil, remove from the heat and set aside.

Put the egg yolks in a large, heatproof bowl. In a separate bowl, combine the remaining sugar and the cornflour/cornstarch and mix thoroughly. Add to the egg yolks and vanilla extract and whisk thoroughly.

While the milk mixture is still hot, whisk it into the egg mixture in the bowl. Strain the mixture back into the saucepan, set over medium–low heat and whisk continuously until it reaches a boil.

Strain the mixture again into a bowl and stir in the butter until melted and thoroughly combined. Lay a sheet of clingfilm/plastic wrap directly on the surface of the pastry cream, then let cool. Refrigerate for 30 minutes before using.

When ready to use, whisk the cream lightly to bring it back to a semi-soft consistency.

cream cheese icing

I always make extra of this icing because it just tastes so good! To lighten the icing, replace half the cream cheese with lebneh, a type of strained yogurt that can be easily found in Turkish and Middle Eastern supermarkets.

180 g/1½ sticks butter, soft
250 g/2¼ cups icing/
   confectioners' sugar
2 tablespoons golden syrup
800 g/1 lb. 12 oz. cream cheese
2 teaspoons vanilla extract

makes enough to frost up to 24 cupcakes or to fill and cover a 20-cm/8-inch cake

Using an electric mixer with paddle or beater attachment (or an electric whisk), beat the butter, sugar and golden syrup until the mixture is lightened in colour and fluffy in texture.

Add the cream cheese and vanilla extract and beat well.

VARIATIONS

MAPLE WALNUT CINNAMON: add an extra 3 tablespoons maple syrup, 1 teaspoon ground cinnamon and 100 g/¾ cup chopped walnuts.

CARDAMOM RUM: add 2 teaspoons ground cardamom, a pinch of freshly grated nutmeg and 3 tablespoons dark rum.

CHOCOLATE AMARETTO HAZELNUT: add 100 g/4 oz. melted dark/semi-sweet chocolate, 2 tablespoons Amaretto and 50 g/⅓ cup chopped hazelnuts.

American vanilla buttercream

Unlike the varied European varieties of buttercream, American buttercream isn't technically a buttercream at all but a frosting consisting of butter and icing sugar to replicate the qualities of real buttercream. It is essential to making archetypal American cupcakes. The milk helps to loosen up the buttercream when you don't want it to be too sweet. Think of sugar as a wet ingredient, so if the icing is still quite stiff but you don't want it to be sweeter, add milk to taste.

350 g/3 sticks butter, soft and cut into chunks

780 g/7 cups icing/confectioners' sugar

30–50 ml/2–3 tablespoons milk

1 tablespoon vanilla extract

makes enough to frost up to 24 cupcakes or to fill and cover a 20-cm/8-inch cake

Using an electric mixer with paddle or beater attachment (or an electric whisk), beat the butter and sugar until the mixture is lightened in colour and fluffy in texture. Stir in the milk and vanilla extract.

If it's not sweet enough, add more icing/confectioners' sugar. If it is too sweet but still stiff, add milk. If it is too sweet and really runny, add soft butter.

VARIATIONS

COCONUT: replace the milk with coconut milk and add 2 teaspoons coconut extract to boost the flavour.

RUM: replace the vanilla extract with dark rum.

MOCHA: add 2 tablespoons espresso and 3 tablespoons cocoa powder.

COOKIES & CREAM: add 200 g/6½ oz. lightly crushed Oreo cookies.

MINT: add 1 teaspoon mint extract and 1 teaspoon green food colouring.

Italian buttercream

This buttercream is luscious, fluffy, silky and sweet. The meringue needs to be cooled down enough to add the butter, otherwise the mixture will melt. If it does, put the mixture in the fridge for an hour and whip again when the butter has solidified.

360 g/1¾ cups caster/
    superfine sugar

1 tablespoon golden syrup

100 ml/½ cup water

6 egg whites

600 g/5 sticks butter, soft
    and cut into big chunks

flavouring of your choice:
    3 teaspoons vanilla
    extract; 1 shot of
    espresso; melted
    chocolate; 1–2 shots of
    Baileys; lemon juice and
    lemon zest; room-
    temperature raspberry
    coulis; slightly warmed
    peanut butter

sugar thermometer

*makes 1 kg/2 lbs.
or enough to frost
24 cupcakes*

Put the sugar, golden syrup and water in a large saucepan and mix until well combined, making sure that no stray grains of sugar remain unmixed. Brush the inside of the saucepan with clean water to dislodge any stray grains. Set over high heat and bring to a rapid boil. When the sugar mixture has come to a boil, add a sugar thermometer and keep cooking until it reaches well into soft ball stage, 120°C/248°F. Remove from the heat.

Put the egg whites in a large, heatproof bowl if using an electric whisk (in which case you will need a second person to help you). Or use an electric mixer with whisk attachment. Whisk the egg whites to soft peaks.

Slowly pour a steady stream of sugar syrup into the egg whites, being careful not to hit the whisk while doing so. Continue whisking until the meringue cools slightly.

Add the softened butter one third at a time and whip until fully incorporated. Stir in the flavouring of your choice. Keeps for up to 1 week at room temperature.

fudge icing

The best showcase of chocolate is when it's paired with cream, either in mousse or truffle form – it's the ultimate expression of a chocoholic's dream. The key to this recipe is the addition of golden syrup to add elasticity and glossiness to the ganache. Pay attention to the stirring; the emulsion is tricky to make, but if you follow the recipe perfectly, you will be successful.

250 ml/1 cup whipping cream

65 g/3 tablespoons golden syrup

350 g/12 oz. good dark/semi-sweet chocolate (we recommend 70%), finely chopped

1 teaspoon vanilla extract

75 g/5 tablespoons butter, cut into cubes and chilled

makes enough to frost up to 24 cupcakes or to fill and cover a 20-cm/8-inch cake

Put the cream and golden syrup in a medium saucepan and bring to a boil.

Put the chocolate in a large, heatproof bowl. As soon as the cream mixture has come to a boil, immediately pour it over the chocolate. Set aside for 1 minute.

Using a small balloon whisk placed in the middle of the bowl, stir with very small motions. Don't stray from the middle of the bowl. You are making an emulsion by taking a large amount of chocolate at the bottom of the bowl and slowly adding small amounts of cream to it. Stirring in larger motions will incorporate more cream than needed, breaking the emulsion and resulting in a dull, grainy mixture. Do not incorporate air, as that will result in unwanted air bubbles and shorten the life of the icing. Keep stirring with small motions – it will look like nothing is happening until eventually a very shiny, thick, glossy mixture forms. Gradually stir in wider motions to incorporate more cream into the emulsion until it's fully combined.

Add the vanilla extract and butter and mix until well combined. Set aside to let the chocolate firm up before using.

cookies & bars

lemon verbena semolina cookies

zest and juice of 1 lemon

½ teaspoon dried lemon verbena tea leaves

200 g/1 cup caster/ superfine sugar, plus extra for dipping

¼ teaspoon salt

110 g/1 stick butter, soft

1½ tablespoons extra virgin olive oil

2 eggs

1 egg yolk

1 tablespoon vanilla extract

280 g/2 cups plain/ all-purpose flour, sifted

140 g/1 cup fine semolina (if you use coarse, add 2 tablespoons plain/ all-purpose flour to absorb more liquid)

1 teaspoon baking powder

¼ teaspoon bicarbonate of/baking soda

baking sheets, lined with parchment paper

makes about 20

Using an electric mixer with paddle or beater attachment (or an electric whisk), mix the lemon zest, tea leaves, sugar and salt, and beat until the sugar smells very lemony – about 1 minute. The sugar will bruise the lemon and tea, releasing the essential oils. Add the butter, olive oil and lemon juice and beat until white and fluffy.

Beat the eggs and egg yolk together in a small bowl. Slowly mix into the butter mixture, beating continuously. Scrape down the batter from the side of the bowl and beat again until thoroughly combined. The mixture should look like a whipped, shiny mayonnaise. Add the vanilla extract and mix.

Mix the flour, semolina, baking powder and bicarbonate of/ baking soda together. Tip into the butter mixture and stir until just combined. The dough will be very soft. Still in the bowl, press it down with clingfilm/plastic wrap to remove any big air bubbles, cover with the clingfilm/plastic wrap and refrigerate for 1 hour.

Preheat the oven to 170°C (340°F) Gas 5.

Pull off pieces of dough the size of golf balls and roll into neat balls with your hands. Dip them thoroughly in caster/superfine sugar and place on the prepared baking sheets, spacing them apart to allow for spreading during baking. Slightly flatten each ball into a disc with the palm of your hand.

Bake in the preheated oven for 12 minutes or until light golden and the tops look dry and matt. Remove from the oven and let cool on the baking sheets for 1 minute. Transfer the cookies to a wire rack and let rest for 20 minutes or until firm to the touch.

snickerdoodles

225 g/2 sticks butter, soft

315 g/1½ cups plus
    1 tablespoon caster/
    superfine sugar

2 eggs

1 teaspoon vanilla extract

350 g/2½ cups plain/
    all-purpose flour

2 teaspoons baking powder

½ teaspoon salt

for dipping

2 tablespoons ground
    cinnamon

300 g/1½ cups caster/
    superfine sugar

*baking sheets, lined with
parchment paper*

makes about 24

Using an electric mixer with paddle or beater attachment (or an electric whisk), beat the butter and sugar until it turns almost white in colour and is light and fluffy.

Slowly incorporate the eggs, one at a time. Scrape down the batter from the side of the bowl and beat for another minute. Add the vanilla extract and mix.

Sift the flour, baking powder and salt together. With the mixer on slow speed, add the flour mixture to the butter mixture. Beat until just combined and a dough forms. Wrap the dough in clingfilm/plastic wrap and refrigerate for 15 minutes.

Meanwhile, mix the cinnamon and sugar, for dipping, in a shallow bowl.

Preheat the oven to 160°C (315°F) Gas 4.

Pull off pieces of dough the size of golf balls and roll into neat balls with your hands. Slightly flatten each ball into a disc with the palm of your hand and dip each thoroughly in the cinnamon sugar. Place on the prepared baking sheets, spaced apart.

Bake in the preheated oven for 13–16 minutes until the edges are slightly golden and the tops look dry and matt.

Remove from the oven and let cool on the baking sheets for 1 minute. Transfer the snickerdoodles to a wire rack and let rest until ready to eat or eat them hot, straight out of the oven.

lavender shortbread

70 g/⅓ cup caster/superfine
  sugar, plus extra for
  sprinkling

2 tablespoons icing/
  confectioners' sugar

½ teaspoon dried lavender

¼ teaspoon fine sea salt

350 g/3 sticks butter,
  slightly soft, cubed

350 g/2½ cups plain/
  all-purpose flour

*brownie/baking pan,
30 x 20 x 5 cm/12 x 8 x
2 inches, baselined with
parchment paper*

makes 24 squares

Preheat the oven to 145°C (290°F) Gas 3.

Whiz both the sugars, the lavender and salt in an electric mixer
with paddle attachment (or rub with your bare hands) until the
lavender buds are bruised and the sugars smell of lavender.

Beat the butter into the sugar mixture until well combined.
Fold in the flour until just combined.

Transfer the mixture to the prepared brownie pan and pat the
dough down until well combined and level. Sprinkle caster/
superfine sugar over the top.

Bake in the preheated oven for 40–55 minutes until the top
is golden brown and the edges shrink from the pan edges.

Remove from the oven and let cool in the pan for 10 minutes.
Remove from the pan and cut into 24 squares.

chocolate peanut butter biscotti

300 g/2 cups plain/all-purpose flour

1½ teaspoons baking powder

1½ teaspoons salt

100 g/½ cup light brown soft sugar

40 g/2 tablespoons natural cocoa powder

40 g/2 tablespoons golden syrup

3 tablespoons sunflower oil

2 eggs

2 teaspoons water

1 teaspoon vanilla extract

80 g/⅔ cup peanuts

80 g/3 oz. good dark/semi-sweet chocolate, finely chopped

caster/superfine sugar, for sprinkling

70 g/½ cup peanut butter

baking sheet, lined with parchment paper

makes about 30

Put the flour, baking powder, salt, sugar and cocoa powder in a large mixing bowl and mix until well combined.

Put the golden syrup, oil, eggs, water and vanilla extract in a separate bowl and whisk until well combined. Add to the dry mixture and mix until just combined and no trace of dry flour remains. Add the peanuts and chocolate and incorporate until just combined. Bring the dough together into a ball, wrap in clingfilm/plastic wrap and refrigerate for 1 hour.

Preheat the oven to 145°C (290°F) Gas 3.

Sprinkle the work surface liberally with caster/superfine sugar. Transfer the dough to the work surface and flatten roughly with your hands. Dot spoonfuls of peanut butter all over the dough. Lightly roll the dough into a log about 6 cm/2½ inches wide and 2 cm/1 inch high (it will spread when baking). Encase the peanut butter inside the log, as it can burn if exposed to the heat of the oven. Place on the prepared baking sheet and bake in the preheated oven for 25–40 minutes until the top is hardened, and when tapped, feels sturdy inside. Remove from the oven and let cool for 30 minutes. Turn the oven temperature down to 135°C (265°F) Gas 2.

Slice the cooled log, diagonally, into 1-cm/½-inch wide batons. Lay all the batons flat on the same baking sheet and bake for 10–15 minutes until dry, then flip all the biscotti over and bake again for 10–15 minutes. Remove from the oven and let cool on the baking sheet for 1 minute. Transfer the biscotti to a wire rack and let cool completely. Store in airtight container for up to 1 month.

nutty lemon biscotti

100 g/½ cup caster/
superfine sugar, plus
extra for sprinkling

zest and juice of 1 large
lemon

350 g/2½ cups plain/
all-purpose flour

1½ teaspoons baking
powder

1½ teaspoons salt

a pinch of ground
cardamom

40 g/2 tablespoons honey

2 eggs

3 tablespoons extra virgin
olive oil

1 teaspoon vanilla extract

50 g/¼ cup shelled, unsalted
whole pistachios

50 g/⅓ cup blanched
hazelnuts

50 g/¼ cup almonds

*baking sheet, lined with
parchment paper*

makes about 30

Whiz the sugar and lemon zest in an electric mixer with paddle attachment (or rub with your bare hands) until the sugar smells tart and lemony. Add the flour, baking powder and salt, and stir until well combined.

Put the lemon juice, ground cardamom, honey, eggs, olive oil and vanilla extract in a separate bowl and whisk until well combined. Add to the dry mixture and mix until just combined and no trace of dry flour remains. Add all the nuts and incorporate until just combined. The dough will be sticky! Bring it together into a ball, wrap in clingfilm/plastic wrap and refrigerate for 1 hour.

Preheat the oven to 145°C (290°F) Gas 3.

Sprinkle the work surface liberally with caster/superfine sugar. Transfer the dough to the work surface and lightly roll or shape it into a log about 6 cm/2½ inches wide and 2 cm/1 inch high (it will spread when baking). Place on the prepared baking sheet and bake in the preheated oven for 25–40 minutes until the top is hardened and, when tapped, feels sturdy inside. Remove from the oven and let cool for 30 minutes. Turn the oven temperature down to 135°C (265°F) Gas 2.

Slice the cooled log, diagonally, into 1-cm/½-inch wide batons. Lay all the batons flat on the same baking sheet and bake for 10–15 minutes until dry, then flip all the biscotti over and bake again for 10–15 minutes. Remove from the oven and let cool on the baking sheet for 1 minute. Transfer the biscotti to a wire rack and let cool completely. Store in airtight container for up to 1 month.

rocky road fudge bars

120 g/⅔ cup caster/
superfine sugar

500 g/4¼ sticks butter,
slightly soft

500 g/3½ cups plain/
all-purpose flour

a pinch of salt

topping

150 g/1¼ sticks butter

100 g/⅓ cup golden syrup

150 ml/⅔ cup whipping
cream

150 g/5½ oz. good dark/
semi-sweet chocolate,
chopped into chunks

500 g/2½ cups caster/
superfine sugar

1 teaspoon vanilla extract

12 large marshmallows

80 g/⅔ cup roasted almonds

*baking pan, 30 x 20 x 5 cm/
12 x 8 x 2 inches, greased and
lined with parchment paper*

sugar thermometer

makes about 24

Preheat the oven to 170°C (340°F) Gas 5.

Beat the sugar and butter until well combined. Fold in the flour and salt until just combined. Transfer the mixture to the prepared brownie pan and pat the dough down until well combined and level. Refrigerate for 5 minutes.

Bake in the preheated oven for 18–25 minutes until the top is golden brown and the edges shrink from the pan. Remove from oven and let cool.

Meanwhile, make the topping. Put the butter, golden syrup, cream, chocolate and sugar into a large saucepan. Add the sugar thermometer and cook over medium heat until the temperature on the thermometer reaches 100°C/212°F. Stir occasionally.

When the mixture looks homogeneous, brush the inside of the saucepan with clean water to dislodge any stray grains of sugar. Keep cooking over medium heat to bring to soft ball stage, 120°C/248°F. When the fudge reaches 120°C/248°F, remove from the heat and pour into a large, metal mixing bowl. Stir in the vanilla extract and continue stirring until the fudge cools down and loses its glossiness. This can take a few minutes.

While still warm and pourable, pour the fudge on top of the shortbread base and let sit for 4 minutes. Chop the marshmallows. Before the fudge completely sets, sprinkle the almonds and marshmallows on top and press in slightly. Let cool completely.

When cool, remove from the pan and cut into 24 small squares.

scones &

small treats

the ultimate scone

600 g/4¼ cups plain/
    all-purpose flour

75 g/⅓ cup caster/superfine
    sugar

¼ teaspoon salt

5 teaspoons baking powder

240 g/2 sticks butter, cut
    into cubes and chilled
    for at least 10 minutes

2 eggs

120 ml/½ cup milk

150 ml/⅔ cup whipping
    cream

*round cookie cutter in the
size of your choice*

*baking sheets, lined with
parchment paper*

makes about 24

Put the flour, sugar, salt and baking powder in a large mixing bowl and stir with a wooden spoon until well combined. Add the cold butter and rub between your fingertips until you reach a sand-like consistency. Refrigerate for 10 minutes.

Put the eggs, milk and cream in a separate bowl and beat lightly. Refrigerate for 10 minutes.

Preheat the oven to 180°C (365°F) Gas 6. Preheating is crucial!

Fold the egg mixture into the sandy flour mixture until just combined and no bits of dryness remain. (As soon as you add any form of liquid to any dough, the flour will automatically want to make gluten with liquids, and the best way to prevent that is to keep the dough from being overworked or warming up.) The dough should be quite wet and, when pulled apart, break off in clumps and not stretch. Refrigerate for 10 minutes.

Flour your work surface and rolling pin liberally. Flip your cold dough on the surface. Don't knead! Liberally flour the top of the dough. Roll the dough to about the height of the cookie cutter you're using. Dip the cutter in flour and use to cut a round from the dough. Transfer to the prepared baking sheet. Continue cutting out rounds, then gather up the off-cuts and gently re-ball and re-roll to cut out more. Bake the scones in the preheated oven for 8 minutes if they are small or 10 minutes if they are big.

Finally, turn the oven down to 170°C (340°F) Gas 5 and bake for another 8–14 minutes or until golden and well risen. Serve warm with clotted cream and strawberry jam on the day of baking.

orange cranberry scones

60 g/5 tablespoons caster/
   superfine sugar, plus
   extra for sprinkling

zest of 1 orange

530 g/3¾ cups plain/
   all-purpose flour

1½ teaspoons baking
   powder

½ teaspoon salt

350 g/3 sticks butter, finely
   chopped and chilled

3 eggs

1 egg yolk

185 ml/¾ cup whipping
   cream

100 g/¾ cup dried
   cranberries

*baking sheet, lined with
parchment paper*

makes about 12

Whiz the sugar and orange zest in an electric mixer with paddle attachment (or rub with your bare hands) until the sugar smells citrussy. Add the flour, baking powder and salt and stir.

Add the cold butter to the flour mixture and rub between your fingertips until you reach a sand-like consistency. Refrigerate for 20 minutes.

Preheat the oven to 170°C (340°F) Gas 5.

Put the whole eggs, egg yolk and cream in a separate bowl and beat lightly. Pour into the sandy flour mixture and add the cranberries. Fold until just combined. Be careful not to overmix at this stage, to ensure the scones stay nice and soft. Keep in mind that the dough will be quite soft and sticky.

Sprinkle the baking sheet liberally with caster/superfine sugar.

Flip the dough out onto the baking sheet and sprinkle caster/superfine sugar over the top. Pat down into a disc about 3 cm/1¼ inches high.

Using a sharp, serrated knife, cut the dough disc into fat wedges like a pie, and space them apart on the baking sheet. Bake in the preheated oven for 25–30 minutes until golden brown and solid when pressed.

Serve warm. Scones are best eaten on the day of baking.

blueberry streusel muffins

225 g/1½ cups plain/
   all-purpose flour, plus
   1 tablespoon extra

200 g/1 cup caster/superfine
   sugar

1½ teaspoons baking powder

¼ teaspoon salt

50 ml/3 tablespoons milk

40 ml/2 tablespoons double/
   heavy cream

2 eggs

65 g/4 tablespoons butter, melted

250 g/2½ cups blueberries

streusel topping

200 g/1½ cups plain/
   all-purpose flour

70 g/⅓ cup dark brown soft
   sugar

70 g/⅓ cup caster/superfine sugar

125 g/1 stick butter, cut into
   cubes and chilled

2 teaspoons ground cinnamon

1 teaspoon vanilla extract

*12-hole muffin pan, lined with
muffin cases*

makes 12

Preheat the oven to 180°C (365°F) Gas 6.

Put the flour, sugar, baking powder and salt in a large mixing bowl and stir until well blended.

In a separate bowl, combine the milk, cream and eggs. Pour into the flour mixture and stir until just combined. Fold in the melted butter.

In another bowl, toss the blueberries in the extra tablespoon of flour until thoroughly coated, then fold into the muffin batter.

Spoon the mixture into the prepared muffin cases, filling them four-fifths of the way up.

To make the streusel topping, combine all ingredients and rub with your fingers until nice crumbly, pea-sized balls form. Refrigerate for 10 minutes.

Scatter the streusel topping over the muffins.

Bake in the preheated oven for 25–35 minutes. A wooden skewer inserted in the middle should come out dry and crumbly, and the tops of the muffins should feel springy to the touch. Remove the muffins from the muffin pan and eat immediately.

almond cherry muffins

240 g/1¼ cups caster/
   superfine sugar

zest of 1 lemon

150 g/1 cup plain/
   all-purpose flour, plus
   1 tablespoon extra

70 g/½ cup ground almonds

2 teaspoons baking powder

a pinch of salt

3 eggs

130 g/½ cup Greek yogurt

½ teaspoon vanilla extract

¼ teaspoon almond extract

80 ml/⅓ cup sunflower oil

50 g/3½ tablespoons butter,
   melted

120 g/1¼ cups pitted sour
   cherries

about 50 g/⅔ cup flaked/
   slivered almonds, for
   sprinkling

*12-hole muffin pan, lined
with muffin cases*

makes 16

Preheat the oven to 170°C (340°F) Gas 5.

Whiz the sugar and lemon zest in an electric mixer with paddle attachment (or rub with your bare hands) until the sugar smells super lemony. Add the flour, ground almonds, baking powder and salt and mix well.

In a separate bowl, combine the eggs, yogurt and vanilla and almond extracts. Pour into the flour mixture and stir until just combined and no traces of flour remain. Fold in the oil and melted butter.

In another bowl, toss the cherries in the extra tablespoon of flour until thoroughly coated, then fold into the muffin batter.

Spoon the mixture into the prepared muffin cases and scatter the almonds over the tops. Bake in the preheated oven for 20–28 minutes. A wooden skewer inserted in the middle should come out dry and crumbly, and the tops of the muffins should feel springy to the touch. Remove the muffins from the muffin pan and eat immediately.

doughnut muffins

420 g/3 cups plain/
  all-purpose flour

4 teaspoons baking powder

½ teaspoon salt

½ teaspoon ground nutmeg

330 g/1⅔ cups caster/
  superfine sugar

2 eggs, lightly beaten

375 ml/1½ cups buttermilk

2 teaspoons vanilla extract

130 ml/⅔ cup sunflower oil

coating & dipping

250 g/2 sticks butter, melted

300 g/1½ cups caster/
  superfine sugar

about ½ jar of raspberry
  jam

*2 x 12-hole muffin pans,
well greased*

*piping bag fitted with a
plain nozzle/tip*

makes about 22

Preheat the oven to 180°C (365°F) Gas 6.

Put all the dry ingredients in a bowl. Add all the wet ingredients and stir until just combined. Don't overmix.

Spoon the mixture into the muffin pan holes, filling them three quarters of the way up.

Bake in the preheated oven for 22–30 minutes. A wooden skewer inserted in the middle should come out dry and crumbly.

While the muffins are baking, put the melted butter and sugar in their own shallow bowls and set aside.

Remove the muffin pans from the oven and tip the muffins out. Immediately dip the muffins in the melted butter, then roll in the sugar to liberally and evenly coat.

Fill the prepared piping bag with jam. Push the nozzle/tip through the top (or bottom if you want it to look neater) of the doughnut, up to midway. Pipe about 1 tablespoon of jam inside each doughnut and serve immediately.

APPLE CINNAMON VARIATION: add ½ teaspoon ground cardamom to the batter, and 2 teaspoons ground cinnamon to the caster/superfine sugar for coating. Fill with apple jam or compote.

devil's food cupcakes

120 g/1 cup natural cocoa powder

250 ml/1 cup boiling water

125 ml/½ cup milk

1½ teaspoons vanilla extract

125 g/1 stick butter, soft

275 g/1⅓ cups dark brown soft sugar

165 g/¾ cup caster/superfine sugar

125 ml/½ cup vegetable oil

4 eggs

280 g/2 cups plain/all-purpose flour

1¼ teaspoons bicarbonate of/baking soda

Fudge Icing (see page 23)

muffin pans, lined with about 24 large cupcake cases

makes about 24 cupcakes

Preheat the oven to 170°C (340°F) Gas 5.

Put the cocoa powder in a bowl. Add the boiling water and mix well. Stir in the milk and vanilla extract and set aside.

Using an electric mixer with paddle or beater attachment (or an electric whisk), beat the butter and both sugars until the mixture is light in colour and fluffy in texture. Slowly pour in the oil in a steady stream and mix until combined. Add the eggs, one at a time, beating until thoroughly combined before adding the next. Scrape down the side of the bowl and mix again.

In another bowl, combine the flour and bicarbonate of/baking soda and sift twice.

Add one third of the flour mixture to the egg mixture and mix until well incorporated. Add half the cocoa/milk mixture and mix until just combined. Repeat with another third of the flour mixture, then the rest of the cocoa/milk mixture. Finally, add the last third of the flour mixture and mix until thoroughly combined.

Spoon the mixture into the cupcake cases.

Bake in the preheated oven for 18–23 minutes. A wooden skewer inserted in the middle should come out with almost no crumbs attached, and the middle of the cupcakes, when pressed, should spring back slightly instead of sink.

Remove from the oven and let cool in the muffin pans for 10 minutes. Transfer to a wire rack to cool for 1 hour. Spread the Fudge Icing over the cooled cupcakes with a spatula.

raspberry meringues

6 egg whites

350 g/1¾ cups caster/
superfine sugar

150 ml/⅔ cup storebought
raspberry coulis, for
painting

*baking sheets, lined with
parchment paper*

makes about 40

Preheat the oven to 110°C (215°F) Gas ½.

Pour water into a large saucepan until one third full and heat
to simmering point over medium–low heat.

Put the egg whites and sugar in a wide, shallow metal bowl and
lightly mix to combine. Sit the bowl over the pan of simmering
water (making sure that the bottom of the bowl doesn't touch the
water) and let the mixture heat up until it is warm to the touch
and the sugar has dissolved. Stir occasionally. Remove from the
heat and whisk with an electric whisk until glossy and stiff peaks
are reached.

Using 2 tablespoons, scoop the mixture into golf-ball sized
meringues onto the prepared baking sheets.

Bake in the preheated oven for 50–60 minutes until firm.
Remove the meringues from the oven. Using a pastry brush, paint
raspberry coulis onto the meringues and put back into the oven to
bake until the coulis has turned a darker, more purpley colour and
the meringue is dry to the touch. The coulis can feel slightly sticky.

Remove from the oven and let cool. Remove from the parchment
paper and store in an airtight container for up to 1 week.

VARIATIONS

PLAIN MERINGUES: add the seeds from ½ vanilla pod/bean to the
egg whites and sugar before heating.

OTHER FLAVOURS: dust cocoa powder or sprinkle crushed
pistachios or desiccated coconut over the meringues before baking.

vanilla marshmallows

20 g/3 tablespoons
   powdered gelatine

120 ml/½ cup cold water

440 g/2¼ cups caster/
   superfine sugar

160 g/½ cup golden syrup

200 ml/¾ cup water

1 tablespoon vanilla extract

pan/cooking spray, for the
   baking pan

cornflour/cornstarch, for
   coating

sugar thermometer

*baking pan, 30 x 20 x 5 cm/
12 x 8 x 2 inches, lined with
parchment paper*

makes 24

Put the gelatine and the 120 ml/½ cup cold water in large mixing bowl and stir. Let sit and all the gelatine to swell or 'bloom'.

Put the sugar, golden syrup and the 200 ml/¾ cup water in a large saucepan and stir to combine. Brush the insides of the saucepan with clean water to dislodge any stray grains of sugar. Bring to a boil, add a sugar thermometer and keep cooking to bring to firm ball stage, 120°C/248°F.

Whisking furiously with an electric whisk (or in an electric mixer), slowly add the sugar syrup to the gelatine mixture. Whisk thoroughly until thick, bubble-gum-like strands form. Stir in the vanilla extract.

Spray everything with pan/cooking spray including spatulas, brownie pan, spoons, hands, etc. to avoid sticking! Spoon the mixture into the prepared brownie pan and spread evenly. Sift some cornflour/cornstarch over the top and let rest for 2 hours.

Using a greased knife, cut the marshmallows into cubes and toss in cornflour/cornstarch. Store in an airtight container for up to 2 weeks.

RASPBERRY VARIATION: reduce the cold water to 60 ml/¼ cup for adding to gelatine. Fold in 60 ml/¼ cup storebought raspberry coulis until streaky. Continue recipe as above. After making and resting for 2 hours, tip the slab of marshmallow out of the pan onto a board, cut into squares and coat in 100 g/4 oz. ground, freeze-dried raspberries mixed with a little cornflour/cornstarch.

cakes

Key lime pie

400 g/14 oz. digestive biscuits/graham crackers

75–100 g/¾–1 stick butter, melted

1½ x 397-g/14-oz. cans of sweetened condensed milk

juice and zest of 13 limes (no, really!)

8 egg yolks

a pinch of salt

whipped cream

400 ml/1⅔ cups double/heavy cream

40 g/⅓ cup icing/confectioners' sugar

1 teaspoon vanilla extract

23-cm/9-inch pie dish/plate, greased and lined with parchment paper

baking beans

serves 8–10

Preheat the oven to 145°C (290°F) Gas 3.

To make the crust, crush the digestive biscuits/graham crackers until you get fine crumbs. Add the melted butter – the amount of butter you will need is variable. Test by grabbing a bit of the mixture and squeezing into your hand to make a ball, then releasing your hand. The mixture should hold its shape, but also fall apart when touched slightly. If it doesn't hold its shape, add more butter, otherwise the biscuit/cracker will dissolve into the cheesecake and you'll have no crust. If it holds its shape too well, add more biscuits/crackers to absorb the butter, otherwise your crust will be too hard. Press the mixture into the pie dish/plate, going all the way up the side. Cover with a round of parchment paper and fill with baking beans to the top. Bake in the preheated oven for 12–20 minutes until the crust is firm and dry. Remove from the oven and let cool.

Adjust the oven temperature to 160°C (315°F) Gas 4.

To make the custard, whisk the condensed milk, lime juice and zest, egg yolks and salt together in a bowl and taste. If it is too tart, add a bit more condensed milk; not tart enough, add more lime juice. Pour into the baked pie shell and put back in the oven for 18–30 minutes until the top is set and the pie barely jiggles in the middle. Remove from the oven and let cool.

To make the whipped cream, combine all the ingredients in a bowl and whisk to stiff peaks. Spread over the pie and refrigerate for 2 hours before serving.

vanilla layer cake

200 g/1¾ sticks butter, soft

½ teaspoon salt

375 g/1¼ cups caster/
superfine sugar

3 eggs, at room temperature

3 egg yolks, at room
temperature

1 tablespoon vanilla extract

275 g/2 cups plain/
all-purpose flour

2 teaspoons baking powder

160 ml/⅔ cup plus
1 tablespoon milk,
lukewarm

whipped cream and
strawberry jam, to serve

icing/confectioners' sugar,
for dusting

*20-cm/8-inch round cake
pan, greased and baselined
with parchment paper*

serves 8–12

Preheat the oven to 170°C (340°F) Gas 5.

Using an electric mixer with paddle or beater attachment (or an electric whisk), beat the butter, salt and sugar until the mixture is almost white in colour, fluffy in texture and the sugar has dissolved.

Slowly mix the whole eggs into the butter mixture, one at a time, beating until thoroughly combined before adding the next. Add the egg yolks, too, and mix well. Add the vanilla extract and mix.

In another bowl, combine the flour and baking powder well, so that the baking powder is thoroughly incorporated, and sift twice.

Add one third of the flour mixture to the egg mixture and mix until well incorporated. Add half the lukewarm milk and mix until just combined. Repeat with another third of the flour mixture, then the rest of the milk. Finally, add the last third of the flour mixture and mix until thoroughly combined.

Spoon the mixture into the prepared cake pan.

Bake in the preheated oven for 28–35 minutes. A wooden skewer inserted in the middle should come out with almost no crumbs attached, and the middle of the cake, when pressed, should spring back slightly instead of sink. Bake for an additional 5–10 minutes if necessary.

Remove from the oven and let cool in the pan for 10 minutes. Slide a table knife around the edge to loosen the cake, then remove from the pan, transfer to a wire rack to cool for 1 hour before cutting in half horizontally and filling with whipped cream and strawberry jam. Dust with icing/confectioners' sugar.

vegan chocolate mousse cake

Vegan Chocolate Cake
  (see page 17)

2 punnets of raspberries

2 punnets of strawberries, hulled and quartered

handful of crystallized violets

chocolate mousse

800 g/1 lb. 12 oz. good dark/semi-sweet chocolate, finely chopped

600 ml/2½ cups hot water

you will also need lots of ice

serves 8–12

To make the vegan chocolate mousse, put the chocolate in a very large, wide heatproof bowl over a saucepan of simmering water (do not let the base of the bowl touch the water). Leave until melted, then stir with a wooden spoon until smooth and glossy.

Pour the hot water into the bowl of chocolate and mix until nice and smooth.

Sit the bowl in a dish filled with ice cubes. Using an electric whisk, quickly whisk the chocolate and water mixture thoroughly and quickly until a stiff mousse forms. If the mousse is too stiff, add a tiny bit of warm water, or better yet, some rum or espresso. If the mousse is too loose, add some more melted chocolate and quickly whisk up again.

Cut the Vegan Chocolate Cake horizontally into 3 layers.

Put one layer on a cake stand or plate. Spread one third of the vegan chocolate mousse over the cake in generous dollops. Arrange raspberries and strawberries over the top.

Repeat this process with a second layer of cake on top of the first layer. Top with the last layer.

Spread the remaining vegan chocolate mousse over the top of the cake and decorate with the remaining berries (or just raspberries) and crystallized violets.

apple Bourbon pecan cake

225 g/2 sticks butter, soft

220 g/1 generous cup
caster/superfine sugar

220 g/1 generous cup dark
brown soft sugar

3 eggs

280 g/2 cups plain/
all-purpose flour

1 teaspoon baking powder

½ teaspoon bicarbonate
of/baking soda

1 teaspoon ground allspice

1½ teaspoons ground cinnamon

1 teaspoon ground nutmeg

¼ teaspoon ground cloves

¼ teaspoon ground ginger

¼ teaspoon ground cardamom

½ teaspoon salt

3 Granny Smith apples

3 tablespoons Bourbon

120 g/1 cup pecans, toasted
and roughly chopped

*20-cm/8-inch round cake pan,
greased and baselined with
parchment paper*

serves 8–12

Preheat the oven to 160°C (315°F) Gas 4.

Using an electric mixer with paddle or beater attachment
(or an electric whisk), beat the butter and both sugars until the
mixture is almost light in colour and fluffy in texture.

Add the eggs, one at a time, beating until thoroughly combined
before adding the next. Scrape down the side of the bowl and mix
again for 1 minute.

In another bowl, combine the flour, baking powder, bicarbonate
of/baking soda, all the spices and salt and sift twice.

Add one third of the flour mixture to the egg mixture and
mix until well incorporated. Repeat with another third of the
flour mixture, then the rest of the flour mixture and mix until
just combined.

Peel and core the apples and cut them into chunks. Pour the
Bourbon over them in a bowl and mix. Fold the apples and pecans
into the cake mixture, then spoon into the prepared cake pan.

Bake in the preheated oven for 55–70 minutes. A wooden
skewer inserted in the middle should come out with almost
no crumbs attached, and the middle of the cake, when pressed,
should spring back slightly instead of sink. Bake for an additional
5–10 minutes if necessary.

Remove from the oven and let cool in the pan for 10 minutes.
Slide a table knife all around the edge to loosen the cake, then
remove from the pan. Transfer to a wire rack to cool for 1 hour.

triple chocolate cake

70 g/2½ oz. dark/semi-sweet
   chocolate, roughly
   chopped

Italian Buttercream (see
   page 22, but follow the
   method opposite)

Chocolate Buttermilk Cake
   (see page 14)

Fudge Icing (see page 23)

honeycomb/sponge candy
   or other candy bars,
   roughly chopped,
   to decorate

serves about 20

To make a chocolate meringue buttercream, put the chocolate in a large heatproof bowl over a saucepan of simmering water. Do not let the base of the bowl touch the water. Leave until the chocolate has melted, then stir with a wooden spoon until smooth. Remove from the heat and let cool to room temperature.

Whisk the cooled, melted chocolate into the Italian Buttercream until thoroughly combined.

Cut the Chocolate Buttermilk Cake horizontally into 3 equal layers. Put one layer on a cake stand or plate. Spread a thin layer of Fudge Icing over it. Now spread a generous layer of the chocolate meringue buttercream over the top.

Repeat this process with a second layer of cake on top of the first layer. Top with the last layer. Spread a thin layer of chocolate meringue buttercream all over the cake with a spatula, making it as smooth and neat as possible. Refrigerate for 1 hour.

A few minutes before you are ready to take the cake out of the fridge to finish decorating, you will need to soften the remaining fudge icing so that it's a pourable consistency. Be careful because it's an emulsion, so it's prone to splitting. Gently warm the icing in a microwave (or in a heatproof bowl over a saucepan of simmering water) for 10 seconds at a time. Keep checking and warming until it is smooth, runny and glossy. Take the cake out of the fridge and carefully pour the icing over it. Let cool and set slightly before decorating with chopped honeycomb/sponge candy or other candy bars.

frangipane raspberry cake

Almond Frangipane Cake
(see page 12)

vanilla-flavoured Italian
Buttercream (see page
22)

1 jar of organic raspberry
jam (I always like to use
organic jam because I
find it has a lower sugar
content than most –
don't settle for less than
55% fruit content)

2–3 punnets of raspberries

*large piping bag fitted with
St. Honoré nozzle/tip*

serves about 20

Cut the Almond Frangipane Cake horizontally into 3 equal layers.

Put one layer on a cake stand or plate. Spread a very thin layer of vanilla-flavoured Italian Buttercream over the cake.

Put a few spoons of the buttercream into the prepared piping bag. Pipe a circular border of buttercream around the cake no closer than 1 cm/½ inch from the edge. This will act as a flooding wall to keep the raspberry jam from seeping out.

Fill the inside of the border with a thin layer of raspberry jam – but no higher than two thirds of the way up the buttercream, otherwise the jam will seep out. Place the second layer of cake on top and refrigerate for 20 minutes to allow the buttercream to set.

Pipe another border of buttercream, as described above, on top of the cake and fill with raspberry jam again. Place the remaining layer of cake on top and refrigerate for 20 minutes.

Spread a thin layer of the buttercream all over the cake.

Fill the prepared piping bag with the buttercream and, starting from the bottom of the cake, pipe feathers up the side of the cake in one fluid motion. Let the feathers go above the height of the cake if needed. Practise on a plate first, if you like!

Top with a mound of raspberries.

index